MY SOUTH

*a collection of spoken-word poems
based on works by Robert St. John*

EDITED BY BRYAN CURTIS

RUTLEDGE HILL PRESS
Nashville, Tennessee
A Division of Thomas Nelson Publishers
Since 1798
www.thomasnelson.com

turnersouth.com

Published by Rutledge Hill Press, a Division of Thomas Nelson, Inc.,
P.O. Box 141000, Nashville, Tennessee 37214.

Photographers: Nathan Bolster, Kyle Christy, Jake Herrle, Mark Hill,
Carl Jones, Frances McBrien, Craig McMahon, Greg Miller, Edward M. Pioroda

Rutledge Hill Press books may be purchased in bulk for educational, business, fundraising, or sales promotional use.
For information, please e-mail SpecialMarkets@ThomasNelson.com.

Library of Congress Cataloging-in-Publication Data

My South : a people, a place, a world all its own / edited by Bryan Curtis.
   p. cm.
   ISBN 1-4016-0217-7
   1. Southern States—Pictorial works.
   2. Southern States—Social life and customs—Quotations, maxims, etc.
   3. Southern States—Biography—Miscellanea. I. Curtis, Bryan
   F210.M9 2005
   306'.0975—dc22

2005009987

Art Direction and Design by Angie Jones, One Woman Show Design.

Printed in Mexico

05 06 07 08 09 — 5 4 3 2 1

PREFACE

Is there still a truly unique Southern culture? Many scholars have pondered this question. John Shelton Reed of the University of North Carolina at Chapel Hill comments, "Is the South still around? People will disagree about that. I come down on the side that yes, it is. It's not what it was even 30 years ago, much less 100 years ago or 150 years. But it's still not the same as everywhere else. We keep reinventing ways to be different."

The southern experience is as diverse as the people who call it home.

In 2003 and 2004 Turner South hit the road, bringing its television shows and most of its network personnel to destinations such as Memphis, Birmingham, Atlanta, Charlotte, and Charleston. The purpose of these events was to develop an eye-to-eye relationship with viewers and to share with them—and capture on film—some truly southern experiences.

In each city, as part of *My South on Tour,* spoken-word competitions were held, bringing together the best spoken-word artists from throughout the South. Given very little guidance, these poets were invited to write and speak about their South.

The response was amazing. Humbling. *My South Speaks,* the spoken-word event, ignited something deep and powerful: the uncontainable desire of southerners to articulate and celebrate their identity. We found that in the South—in *my* South—the stories still spin.

In this book and on the accompanying DVD, you will find some of the best of the *My South Speaks* spoken-word artists, and perhaps learn something new about *your* South.

My South, the book, speaks to the importance of keeping alive our traditions, be they pilgrimages, marriages, funerals, loyalties, rivalries, football, or food. The poets who appear in these pages understand that behind these traditions lies a uniquely southern spirit. As former *Harper's* editor and Mississippi native Willie Morris observes, "Perhaps in the end, it is the old, inherent, devil-may-care instinct of the South that remains in the most abundance and will sustain the South into its future. The reckless gambler's instinct that fought and lost that war, "Snake" Stabler calling a bootleg play on fourth down. It is gambling with the heart, it is a glass menagerie, it is something that won't let go."

The spoken-word artists of *My South* have found their calling: to reveal the promise of a place where progress comes, but not at the expense of humanity.

MY SOUTH

My wife and I attended a food and wine seminar in Aspen a few years back. Seated with us were two couples from Las Vegas. When one of the women found out that we owned a fine-dining restaurant in Mississippi, she snickered. She exclaimed, "Mississippi doesn't have fine-dining restaurants." I wanted to defend my state and my restaurant with a fifteen-minute soliloquy and public relations rant that would change her mind. It was at this precise moment that it dawned on me—my South is the best-kept secret in the country. Why try to win this woman over? She might move down here! I am always amused by Hollywood's interpretation of the South. We are still, on occasion, depicted as a collective group of sweaty, stupid, backwards-minded, racist rednecks. The South of movies and TV, the Hollywood South, is not my South.

My South is full of honest, hard-working people.
My South is color-blind. In my South, we don't put a premium on pigment. No one cares whether you are black, white, red, or green with orange polka dots.
My South is the birthplace of blues, jazz, and rock 'n' roll. It has banjo pickers and fiddle players, but it also has B. B. King, Muddy Waters, the Allman Brothers, Emmylou Harris, and Elvis.
My South is hot.
My South smells of newly mown grass.
My South was creek swimming, cane-pole fishing, and bird hunting.
In my South, football is king and the Southeastern Conference is the kingdom.
My South is home to the most beautiful women on the planet.
In my South, soul food and country cooking are the same thing.
My South is full of fig preserves, corn bread, butter beans, fried chicken, grits, and catfish.
In my South, we eat foie gras, caviar, and truffles.
In my South, our transistor radios introduced us to the Beatles and the Rolling Stones at the same time they were introduced to the rest of the country.
In my South, grandmothers cook a big lunch every Sunday.
In my South, family matters, deeply.
My South is boiled shrimp, blackberry cobbler, peach ice cream, banana pudding, and oatmeal cream pies.
In my South, people put peanuts in bottles of Coca-Cola and hot sauce on almost everything.
In my South, the tea is iced, and almost as sweet as the women.
My South has air-conditioning.
My South is camellias, azaleas, wisteria, and hydrangeas.
My South is humid.
In my South, the only person who has to sit in the back of the bus is the last person who got on the bus.
In my South, people still say "yes ma'am," "no, ma'am," "please," and "thank you."
In my South, we all wear shoes . . . most of the time.

My South is the best-kept secret in the country. Please continue to keep the secret.

—*Robert St. John*

Jake Herrle/Turner South

In my South, corn bread is magic and must be conjured in a cast-iron skillet and come out yellow, soft, and sweet, but not too soft and not too sweet. In my South, we rhapsodize about homegrown vegetables like yellow squash and sweet onions cooked with salt and pepper and butter or ham fat according by case and availability. The pot likker is almost as good as in field peas or baby butter beans, but you don't need corn bread to sop it up, just eat it with a spoon. My South is a thick, round slice of red tomato as big as the bread, and accompanied only by mayonnaise. In my South, there is nothin' better than a tomato sandwich on a summer evening, then sitting back to watch the shrimp boats and the stars.

—*Rebecca Fir Ivester*

My South is *a state of grace.*

My South is the place where I learned how to spell from reading
the name tags on Grandma's annual flowers.

Where your nearest neighbor may be two miles away, but the moment that
you sneeze or strain to breathe they hear it and rush to your door with
the salve to soothe and onion soup—because onion soup cures everything.

Where hurricanes are just the ocean's way of dealing with depression
and cornfields provide the best shoulders 'cause they're always looking
for someone to listen to.

Where suburban sprawl is a park full of bricked-in mobile homes
with paved driveways and above-ground swimming pools in the back.
And that's all the house that we need because we know that the home
is defined by the heart that resides inside.

Where weeping willows still hold silent vigil over cemeteries filled
with people who were taken way too soon at the age of ninety-five.

This is the place where all you have are your hands and your name,
so you better learn to use both of them wisely.

—*Stacey W. Smallwood*

In my South, *'round here* is an exact location.

My South is one big neighborhood watch— not the official kind. It's just nosy old women sitting on their front porch, sipping sweet tea brewed in the summer heat, swapping stories about their grandkids.

—*Melody Cook*

In my South,
GETTING CALLED BY YOUR FIRST AND MIDDLE NAME WHEN YOU ARE YOUNG IS NEVER A GOOD THING.

My South is church on Sunday—all day long.
Preach! Go on child and sing your song!
Sister in the corner having herself a spell.
Brother deacon on the front row talkin' about . . . well.
Chicken fried and potato salad and fresh snap beans.
Sweet tea, hot sauce, and silver queen.
Peach cobbler on the front porch swattin' flies.
Granddaddy playin' checkers and tellin' lies.
Peach pies and tellin' lies.

—*Michael Evans*

My South has *big families* where everyone remembers everyone else's birthday.

15

In my South,
daughters have been known
to fight over an
heirloom deviled egg plate.

My South is where it is a yard sale, not a garage sale, not a tag sale—that advertises an 8 a.m. start but really starts at 5:30 in the morning when that first car pulls up, knocks on the door askin' why's nothin' set out yet.

—*Ben Smith*

My South is a tree comforting me.

Its ivory velvet blooms emitting

fragrances of exotic places.

Lemon verbena fondly familiar from

sea islands to grand plantations.

Standing through centuries of

hurricanes and sultry evenings

silhouetted by the Carolina moon.

—*Carol Furtwangler*

My South is *azalea and magnolia trees, and kudzu and daylilies.*

In my South,
we all wear shoes—
most of the time.

My South stops on the front-porch stoop to catch breath and say grace,
and see what's going on with the neighbors.
The air swells here, thick as an oak's armchair.
But the bells ring clear—I'm home.
As the marsh melts in my eyes and nose,
the pungent smell basking in this land's glow, masking my heart's flow.
I breathe in deep, and believe in peace and know—I'm home.
The croak of the crickets licks my eardrums with those tiny ticks
and hums of gospel choir flies.
The blues rift on the lyre, slide-slowing down to a different beat.
The one where people say hello in the street to passers-by,
and I know why they call it hope—I'm home.
Grandmother's goose down, a line-dried smocked gown.
The fact that I'm shocked how here, year by year,
the shackles and chains of our history remain near and lift us up.
Our past of shame and fear, now we're tied by our pride.
Bound in the tide, closer to find our color-blind eye.
Scuppernong wine, Frogmore Stew.
How do you put your whole life in a bucket of words
to describe all you've ever known and call it home?
I pull out pecan pie, sweet potato, Mee-maw's smile,
Alice Walker's Sunday chats, wisteria.
I pull out a creole dish from New Orleans.
My South—a rosebush with thorn wings.

—*Frances Lucille Barrett*

In my South,
your word is your bond
and your Sunday shoes shine
like a *good family name.*

In my South, we know where we come from.

Our ancestors are much more than names.

Every year my family gathers at the cemetery plot to pay their respects with

fabricated flowers and fond memories.

From the cemetery we proceed to a nearby park for cold Coke and crispy

chicken, biscuits thick with blackberry jam and butter—and baked beans.

The elms around the picnic table are ablaze with autumn.

The gold and crimson, rich brown leaves

whisper against each other in the welcomed breeze.

In the South, we relish our cool months,

when the earth can finally catch its breath after the long summer heat—

over the final burst of colorful brilliance, settle down to rest for the winter.

My cousins swing on a tire hung from an enormous sheltering oak.

They climb up twisted branches that reach out to embrace the world like

Mama's arms.

—Ashley Pope

In my South, there are no old plantation homes
and girls do not have coming-out parties—but it is the South.
My great-grandmother did not protect her hands from the
sun with lace gloves
or sip mint juleps in the late afternoon—
but she was a fine southern lady,
just a different breed.
Mountain people, we are called.
My ancestors may have had rough exteriors coupled
with harsh accents—
but they had their stubborn moments,
and honor was their lifeblood.

—*Brittany Tocher*

My South is
the *hello,*
the *pardon me,*
the *thank-you,*
or the *yes ma'am.*

25

My South gave you George Wallace and Dr. King.

And my South still has that dream.

My South is my daddy gettin' up at five o'clock every mornin'—

climbin' into a log truck and workin' like a dog past dark every night

at seventy-five years old.

My South is still callin' her "Mama" after all these years—

and not thinking nothin' of it.

My South is homemade peach ice cream, cakewalks and square dances,

cookin' a pig for the Fourth of July

and a mountain of casseroles after my brother's funeral.

My South takes care of her own.

My South is freeways *and* dirt roads.

Pig pickin's *and* gourmet cuisine.

MerleFest *and* Spoleto.

My South revels in our contradictions and is never *ever* short on style.

—*John Givens Hartness*

Edward M. Pioroda/Turner South

MY

SOUTH

IS THE

RHYTHM

OF ITS

LEGENDS.

In my South, Georgia pines make the air smell sweet.

You'll find turtles sunnin' on a cypress log, mud oozin' beneath your feet.

The mornin'll give you grits and gravy, coffee pot, eggs, and sausage meat.

Crumpled corn—a calf is born.

A sleepy southern street.

In my South, we have cotton fields—white cotton fields that climb up over the rise.

All the old folks and the little children are shooin' away the flies.

The dinner bell'll bring collard greens and black-eyed peas, fatback and some pie.

Southern streets and sweltering heat. Southern summer sighs.

In my South, we have "y'alls" and coveralls.

Prayer meetin's at the campground.

Wide-brimmed hats at the pond and cane poles bendin' down.

Supper might be dirty rice and catfish stew and corn bread all around.

Southern sighs and fireflies. Hooowling southern hounds.

In my South, we have starry skies that light up the Milky Way.

Breezes on the veranda that make your hammocks sway.

A midnight snack be a chicken leg, some melon or tea.

Then those howlin' hounds will wake the town to another southern day.

—*Edward Jack Smith*

In my South,
crickets and bullfrogs are my lullaby.

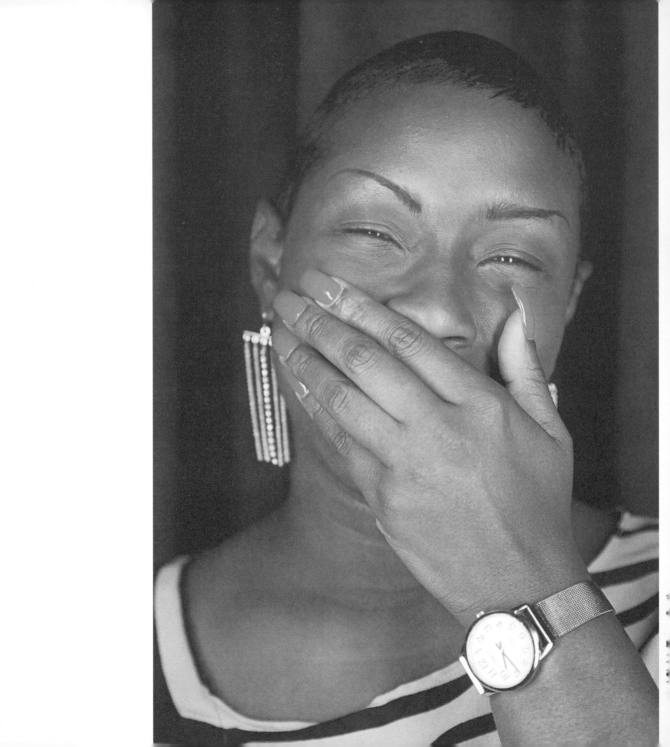

In fall, my South is Thanksgivin' with the upstate cousins.

It's blond wheat fields, clapboard farmhouses, crated cotton.

It's my uncle Johnny givin' thanks for the livin' and the goin'

and my cousin Holmes tellin' a tall one about the turkey we're fixin' to eat.

Now, I don't know why they call slow people "turkeys."

A turkey's a smart bird.

Now this one in particular, I must have tracked him for three years.

Seriously. Smart bird.

I think he graduated Chapel Hill or somethin'.

Smart one.

—*Charlie Geer*

My South is that slow southern slang
that rolls off the tongue
like sweet molasses and
greets every soul we pass as though
we've known them for years.

In my South, black mothers bake our love into
biscuits and hot-water corn bread and say you're
special with lemon cakes and lemonade
while the radio switches between gospel and jazz
as the rhythm and blues seeps through our pores.
Stars take the witness stand and weep their approval
of our collard-green dreams.

In my South, mothers look the past straight in the eye
and own ourselves with a payment in blood and tears—
libations to our ancestors weeping through
every atrocity and every joy.
We are our own allies.

—Valerie Richmond Davis

My South is my testimony.

My South is a song whispering to me from

coastal waters through salt marshes of this

low country, a refrain repeating, "You are home."

Constant in the ocean waves breaking on

solitary strands echoed in the rhythm of the

dolphins rollicking in surf.

My South is a word welcoming me,

a foreigner from the north.

Expressed in dulcet tones still reminiscent of

the accent English men and women brought

four hundred years ago to settle this benign

peninsula at the confluence of the Ashley and

the Cooper rivers to form the Atlantic Ocean.

—Carol Furtwangler

Veer

My South is bare feet dangling over the dock.

My South is a place
where I learned to *slow down*
in order to *keep up.*

My South brings memories of a time when ponytails were donned on the heads of little girls and three pairs of colorful socks were the norm.

Jump rope was always a contest.

Picnics were catered by the candy lady, servin' pickles with peppermint sticks.

Playin' hide-and-go-seek until the lightnin' bugs gave us away.

Screamin'—"Ice in a glass!" "Kool-Aid!" and "Marco Polo!"

We *had* baby fat, not wearing Baby Phat.

All the kids in the neighborhood knew each other, got mad at each other, played with each other, switched girlfriends and boyfriends with each other—and that was cool.

And in the South everybody's mama was "Mama."

And when it was dinnertime, whosever yard you were in—

that's where you ate.

Erica Dunlap

My South is palmetto trees in the moonlight.

Resurrection fern on the outstretched limbs of a live oak.

Wispy curls of Spanish moss draped from a dogwood tree.

It's a trip to the beach with my grandson on a winter day.

A starfish found at the ocean's edge.

A search for sand dollars at low tide.

Shrimp boats as they dock on Shim Creek.

—Frances Pierc

Mark Hill/Turner South

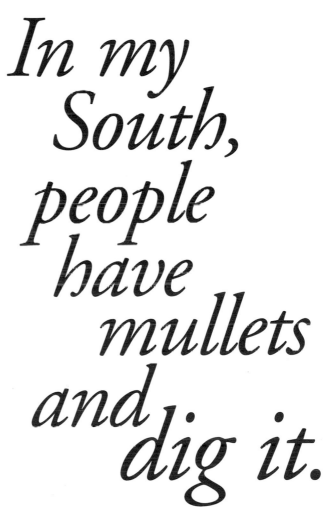

In my South, people have mullets and dig it.

My South is a peace abiding in me offering her song of silence,

her word of welcome, her tree of comfort, her sky of spirits, her

peace of living where I belong, despite my birthplace.

Knowing all along this is my heritage.

This is my home.

—Carol Furtwangler

*In my South,
secrets are heirlooms
and politeness
is a way of life.*

My South is the sound of crickets in the summer, and the sun shining down on Sundays spent swinging on a porch as southern belles strut by with hats that stretch toward the sky. And the streets are grounded with history's seeds sunken deep within the sidewalks.

They've sprouted into sweet tea and meat-and-threes and *thank-you-ma'ams* and *please*.

My South's duality is hostility and hospitality.

It's a song only sung with a southern drawl by a chorus of people who say the word *y'all* and whose lives are rooted in spirituality.

—*Marcus Amiker*

In my South, a man never cusses in the presence of a lady.

In my South, we know the difference between
surviving and truly living.
Around here to be rich means to never go hungry,
so you'll find food, and love, and
opportunity a'plenty,
and there'll be people telling you to pull up
that extra chair that always seems to be handy
and to make yourself at home at the table that
overflows with wisdom and corn bread.
And we'll quench your thirst with sun tea—
made sweet and made cold and served best in
jelly glasses and Mason jars, if you please.

—*Tressy McMillian*

In my South, we are proud to be southern.

My South is day after day of unrelenting sunshine,

followed by the unexpected outburst of a tropical storm.

It's the taste of a peach picked straight from the tree.

Strawberries and asparagus gathered from a backyard garden.

Jam made from blackberries grown in the wild.

It's tomato sandwiches, ripe cantaloupes, and homemade ice cream in summertime.

Coconut cake and pecan pie.

The syrupy sweetness of iced tea.

It's oyster roasts and big bowls of chili on a winter afternoon.

It's the December harvest of the only lemon that survived the frost.

—*Frances Pierc*

My South is where *it's supper*, not dinner.

47

We're still good neighbors in my South.
If you go away for a couple of weeks, we'll pick up your
mail for you, feed your dogs and cats, water your garden,
and when the kudzu swallows your house, we'll all pitch in
to pull away the vines . . . soon as you come home.
We haven't forgotten how to be polite.
We pass the time of day, even in long lines at
the grocery store—much to some people's dismay.
There are some women who stare when old men
call them "ma'am" or "miss."
But even those old men are still called "boys"
by their wives and mothers.
These same women can curse you in a second when they
say, "Ain't that nice" and "Whatever you say, dear—
I'm sure you're right."

—*Chuck DeVarennes*

In my South, sometimes our sentences do end in prepositions—*get over it.*

My South just sits back and relaxes and devours the fruits of her labor.

She watches while conversations are being held between neighbors.

She sits quietly at the Sunday dinner table, mouth watering during
prayer for Big Mama's fried chicken, candied yams, collard greens,
macaroni and cheese, and corn bread.

She turns hands of "double dutch" for the neighborhood girls
and refuses to get upset when she loses her turn.

She braids her brother's hair on the front porch in cornrows
and giggles at her crazy grandmother waving at folks—
that she don't even know.

She enjoys sips of sweet tea under a shady tree
because she knows that sweet tea ain't universal—
you can just ask them folks from New York.

She plays hide-'n-go-seek,
and she's never too busy to speak and meet new sets of eyes when
walkin' down the street.

—Bridgette (Bree) Betts

IN MY SOUTH, YOU WERE TAKEN TOO SOON, NO MATTER HOW OLD YOU WERE WHEN YOU DIED.

The South—its rhythm is inside me.
Hot, sweaty, dusty roads that lead to fields filled with
southern dreams and streams.
As the sun beams down to touch the earth and awaken
the honeysuckles,
I chuckle with the thought of the South.
It's where I've lived most of my life—
with barbecues and fish fries,
growin' up hearin' Uncle June Bug tellin' lies.
There's a church on every corner—
we're known as the Bible Belt.
Growing up, the belt is what I felt.
It helped.

—*Zanya Hammond*

*In my South, the COGIC
ladies wear fantastic hats.*

I'm talkin' about a southern girl—greatest natural wonder of the world.
She's the reason the seasons change.
Her twang, soft as spring rain, is used to soothe pain.
Her silky drawl gives her the ability to touch you even when she says "y'all.
She can be as fierce as a summer storm,
yet on a cold night, her apple-butter eyes can make you feel warm.
Because God has a handle on her life, her soul lights its own candle.
Full of sass, created her own class.
Her champagne smile can calm the wildest beast.
Her smooth caress can bring about the sweetest peace.
As she steps into a room with effortless grace,
her very presence radiates any place.
Men have fought to keep such an appealing treasure—
diamonds, pearls, gold, nothin' can match or measure.

—*Collette De*

*In my South, we don't understand
why anyone would use
one syllable to say something
when two sounds so much nicer.*

55

My South is *overalls and dirt on your knees.*

My South. I'm just gonna tell you how it is.

My South is southern rock 'n' roll, a fishin' pole at the waterin' hole,

barefoot and blue jeans.

My South is shaggin' in the sand.

My South is a rebel *yell.*

My South is a southern belle.

My South is tubin' and cruisin'.

My South is pickin' and grinnin'.

My South is peaches in the summertime and apples in the fall,

an ice cold beer and football on Friday nights, baseball underneath the lights,

barbecue and Sunday school, chasin' girls around the pool.

My South is a Sun Drop when it's really hot, a thunderstorm at five o'clock.

It's trick-or-treat around the block.

My South is you, my South is me.

My South is my friends, my South is my family.

—Andrew Taylor

In my South,
people make time.

Once there was a dreamer in my South—

who dreamed for all mankind.

For all the forgotten people, all those left behind.

And he carried his dreams from the small towns and the cities

to the steps of the Lincoln Memorial.

And he told us of a day when all mankind

would be free at last.

But there are those who out of ignorance and hate

would destroy the dream.

And he was shot down in Memphis around suppertime,

but the dream did not die.

For you can kill the dreamer, but you can't kill the dream.

It lives on in that place where dreams become real.

In that place, the soul is revealed and dreams become real.

—*Kodac Harrison*

In my South, there were mothers in aprons
with pitchers of red Kool-Aid at the back door.
And there were neighborhood swimmin' pools
with blue-mouthed kids runnin' this way
and that way with snow cones in their hands.
My brother and I, we knew respect,
using *ma'am* and *sir* like it was sales tax.
And we were always careful to leave the room
when the adult talking got serious.
In my South, *fixin' to* and *done did* were opposites
and *y'all* was the hallmark of the southern soul.

—Sean Scapaletto

In my South,
down yonder is a
measurement

61

My South is debutantes in lily white bell-shaped ball gowns and gentlemen in white gloves.

My South is an old South.

My South is Dixie two-lane road, peaceful as can be,

laid so very carefully to save every possible tree.

There are people fishin' from a wooden bridge, just as happy as can be.

Not a single sign of frustration on their faces can I see.

I'm on a Dixie ride to yesterday and everywhere I see,

just another sign of another time that keeps on callin' to me.

A time of peace when the world was well,

a time, a time of a southern belle.

Well, there's grand old houses standin' tall with rockers leanin' against the wall,

retaining all of their beauty still, as if possessed by their builder's will.

Songs of birds and a gentle breeze fill the mighty old oak trees,

which if they could, surely would, make yesterday understood.

Clear blue skies and a setting sun, sailboats makin' their final run,

o'er the ocean coming to the shore as it always has before.

Memories of yesterday. "Here today" meant always to stay—

within the view of the very few, who take the time to see.

I'm on a Dixie ride to yesterday and everywhere I see

just another sign of another time that keeps on callin' to me.

A time of peace when the world was well,

a time, a time of the southern belle.

—Paul Samuels

My South is the sting of ocean water on skeeter bites.
Pickin' the banjo on long summer nights.
Payin' the compliment at just the right hour.
Pickles—dill, I like mine sour.
Tellin' stories and makin' up jokes.
Callin' all carbonated beverages Coke.

My South says, "Hey son, slow down, you'll live a little longer!"
Fireworks on the Fourth and collards on New Year's Day.
My South is dreamt of when I'm away and welcomes me
every spring with the most beautiful azaleas you'd ever see.
My South has many colorful characters,
but which color they are doesn't matter to me.
I see society's insecurities but—I feel free.

—*Miles Pittman*

In my South,
we put peanuts in bottles of Coke.

My South is simple, with southern belles and cotton fields and cattails.

Front porch swings and old dirt roads with big city dreams—and my granny's biscuits.

A silky, southern drawl with lightning bugs and overalls.

An afternoon day with sweet tea.

My South is beautiful and it remembers plantation days

and "Amazing Grace," mosquito nets, and a big hoop dress, and a low-country sunset.

Where church bells still sing and houses are housed with full *y'all's* and *ma's* and *pa's*,

and you all know what that means.

It's the sweetest after-dinner pie.

—*Denei Daniel*

In my South, *The Andy Griffith Show* is on at least half a dozen times a day, and that's the way it should be.

In my South, little kids still climb trees, get scrapes on their knees, and say their grace before they eat.

In my South, there's still a candy lady's house with penny candies and quarter popsicles and fifty cents is the price for a pickle—not a rapper.

In my South we go to church and you better not get up out your seat, because we know if we get caught at the neck our butts is good and beat.

—*Odyssey*

In my South, *you give up your seat* to the elderly on the bus.

My South is church revivals in big tents with funeral-home hand fans. Ministers who are more like actors with their dramatics— scaring you right into the pearly gates.

—Melody Cook

IN MY SOUTH,

YOU NEVER

GO TO A FUNERAL

HOME WITHOUT A

COVERED DISH.

In my South, you respect your elders.

They have the wisdom of experience, and

patience born from a lifetime of trials.

Besides if you don't, they'll beat your tail

with a Hot Wheels track and put you

out in the garden pullin' weeds.

I couldn't tell you a story about the

South—the South is too complicated.

Too simple, too urban, too rural.

The South is too old, too new—

to be told by one person.

But my South, that's a story I can tell.

—*David Bird*

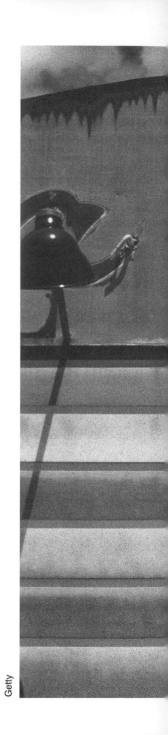

Getty

In my South, you sit in lawn chairs in the back of a pickup at the drive-in.

ELLEN's SOUL FOOD SANDWICHES

$1.85 Hamburger Double-meat $2.85
$1.95 Cheeseburger Double-meat $2.95
$3.00 Pork Chop Sandwich Bar B Q Rib $350
$275 Bar B Q Shoulder Sandwich
$250 Fried Chicken Sandwich Hot Dog Special $365
$125 2 Hot Dogs Ham and Cheese $225
$125 French Fries (small 85) Fried Okra $125 (small 85)
Smoke Sausage $185

YOU!

ELLENS SOUL FOOD & BO MENU

PORK RIBS BONES
SAND   350   3
DINNER   5 50   3
ORDER   8 00   6
SLAB   14 50
SHOULDER 275
RIB TIPS 375

BEEF RIBS BONES
SAND   400   3
DINNER   550   3
ORDER   900   6
SLAB   1500

Enjoy Coca-Cola

THANKS

BLUESMAN'S LEGACY

In my South, *everything* tastes better fried.

In my South, there is a spirit, a holy spirit that
heals old wounds, melts the heart,
and brings all people together.
It's that spirit that is the source of our progress.
We are moving—we are moving forward, you know.
And now that we are moving and
we've got all this progress and that's great.
But you know, I can still have my front porch,
my sweet tea, and that good home cookin'—
even on a low-carb diet.
We can hold on to the beauty of this
old, old place, as we're moving.
We are moving forward, and we are
moving forward together.

—Christine Carr

In my South, we have many traditions—from shrimp and grits

to homemade sweet potato biscuits hot from outta grandma's kitchen.

Festivals that range from art and culture to wildlife expositions.

Believe me, my South covers the whole spectrum on southern tradition.

Some positive and some negative, but still we think free.

See, if there's anything to learn it is to open the arms to receive all things

and give all things—be it joy and pain, tears and smiles, hatred and blood.

—Harold Singletary

My South thinks white sheets are for sleeping on— *not for hiding hatred under.*

...UNTIL JUSTICE ROLLS DOWN LIKE WATERS
AND RIGHTEOUSNESS LIKE A MIGHTY STREAM

MARTIN LUTHER KING JR

My South remembers weekly camp meetings. Kerosene lamps illuminating the brown voices of the elders as they stretch their worn, wrinkled, calloused hands to Jesus and exclaim, "Look where he brought me from to! I don't believe he brought me this far to leave me!"

—*Tiffany Glover*

My South is
healing from its history and
growing from its grief.

My South.

The words "my South" spark nostalgia

at the thoughts of my past, when everyone watched the six o'clock news and sixty miles

per hour was just too fast.

You was ballin' if you had a watch and

"big time" if you had a bike to ride on.

Your palm pilot was your list of chores you had to do before you got to go outside.

Dodge ball and patty-cake taught hand-eye coordination.

And cell phones were useless because moms always knew your location.

Conflicts were solved with fists, not revolvers.

And the colors you wore represented what

was on sale at the mall.

I'm talking about a time when a spankin'

and a hug *meant* somethin'.

When "check yes, no, or maybe" meant lovin'.

When "you better wait

'til your daddy come home" meant punishment.

—*The Minister*

In my South, when moms tell kids not to be ugly, it doesn't have anything to do with their appearance

In my South, you can still find the
middle of nowhere.

My South is a five-pound bigmouth
on an early purple worm.
My South is bobolinks and twelve-point bucks,
from Daytona Beach to Durham.
See, I'm a Tarheel born, and a Tarheel bred,
and when I die, I'm a Tarheel dead.
My South will rise, but not again,
'cause you can't go back where you've never been.
But on this one thing you can depend,
that my Civil War ain't over,
and to God's ear to my mouth I'm glad
I live in the land of cotton.
Ol' times here are not forgotten
and I will not look away—not today.
I'm here to stay.

—*Michael Evans*

Mark Hill/Turner South

83

My South, it isn't on the Interstate.
Those only take you from one place to another
without really seeing a damn thing.
Nope, my South is off of the highway.
That's right! It's the brick storefronts, the diners, the parks
dedicated to little people who did big things in their little pond.
A Main Street where neighbors know each other by name;
who have an account at the store around the corner.
Where a hook—not a lock—keeps the wind from
swingin' that screen door.
Where a town is famous just because its name is
painted large on the water tower.

My South is stretched wide from the Appalachian mountains—
with apple-crisp apples, waterfalls, and sliding rocks—
to the Carolina coast leading us there with peaches and
boiled peanuts, into Charleston with magnolias meant for
climbin'—kissin' beneath.
And plantation oaks hanging so low that
they go under and come back up—just like the Loch Ness monster.
And where Spanish moss drapes around the trees.

—Jessica Deltac

MY SOUTH IS
BARBECUE
AND
POTATO
CHIPS
POOLSIDE
ON THE
FOURTH
OF JULY
AND THE
AMERICAN
FLAG
SNAPPING
IN THE
WIND.

My South has always been the land that time forgot.
Where welcome signs are cypress trees that cradle the cranes and
mockingbirds, and chickweed blankets over moccasin-rich waters.
Where tobacco juice sticks to you like a hazy, hot, humid
forehead kiss from Aunt Cora, who swears you're growing like a weed
but only sees daffodils and lilies in your smile.
Where the wind wears sweet william cologne
that the rain can't wash away.
This is the place that dirt roads ring like doorbells signaling
Sunday evening social time, while the children enjoy mud pies
that took all day to bake.

—*Stacey W. Smallwood*

In my South, the Ryman will always be the home of the Grand Ole Opry.

My South is
front porch
sitting,
screen door
cricking,
constant
finger licking,
guitar picking,
humidity
dripping,
lemonade
sipping,
sweet summer
afternoons.

My South has storms.

Great jagged bolts of lightning.

Thunder cracking like the whips of feral gods.

Hurricanes as big as Texas,

dumber than the dumbest ox and muscled for destruction,

able to wreck the best of homes and leave the tender gardens gross with mud.

But soon enough the sun comes out.

Birds find their way back to business and to song.

Blossoms knowing nothing of their beauty reappear and tempt the bees and butterflies.

There's innocence enough in all the want.

The winds change dreams.

Mud stiffens.

Neighbors wander over.

The air is sweet again, and ripe with what might happen next.

—*Denny Styles*

In my South, the mountains catch the sounds of mothers praying, and the echoes bounce into heaven as mothers prophesy deliverance for their children.

The hums sound the same whether in Baptist churches or on boulevard bars while some mother's son skips a beat, while some dad's girls jump rope with sassy feet, on southern city sidewalks from Jackson to Birmingham.

And children sing the history of their elders from Memphis to Atlanta.

In my South, mothers use their hearts as their weapons of mass instruction, raise their arms to hug their children, caress their loves, embrace this world.

—Valerie Richmond Davis

*In my South, grandmothers
        pass around pictures of
grandbabies and argue about
        the best azalea fertilizer.*

My South is filled with the click-clacks of inner-city baseball bats,

Sunday morning church bells, and fabulous church hats.

All day porch chats and little kids playing "pitty-pat, baker's man"—

the place where the southern belle and her companion is the gentleman.

The place where people had to struggle and fight,

hosed and bit by dogs in the name of civil rights.

Please, oh Lord, will you hear their plight?

They pray on their knees to you every night.

—*Brandon Stuckey*

In my South, black and white people *get along.*

My South is dogwoods shading azaleas that hug
chicken wire along dirt roads.
Dust kicking from back tires of pickups—
old and red, passed father to son.
Generations driving parallel to grassy train tracks
abandoned back when locomotives burned coal
and engineers wore the heat like a tattoo.
They flew past acres of white cotton.
Now green hills roll where sharecroppers used to bend.
Gospel still echoes from leaning shacks behind
the fishing hole—roof gone, dirt floor, planks of wood
resting in the creek, nails rusting in the water that
trickles like crickets in the kudzu.
And banjos pickin' on the back porch sittin' in a rockin' chair
sippin' sweet tea watchin' hounds chase butterflies—
among the milkweeds.

—*Brian Lebrazer*

My South uses knives and forks,
  but biscuits and corn bread finish the job.

My South is where the phrase "Hey y'all watch this!" might be the last words you ever hear from that person. My South is knowin' that wherever I go I can pick up at least three country music stations on my radio. My South is stately large single row houses that have seen centuries of the best and the worst of human nature. My South is a sense of both loss and pride, ingrained in a culture that was too poor to paint and too proud to whitewash. My South is where the Civil War still rages over eastern and western barbecue.

—*Ben Smith*

My South is tailgating on a Saturday afternoon.

My South is sweet-lick penny candy stretched from Savannah and Tupelo, New Orleans and Baton Rouge, to Memphis and Birmingham.
My South speaks of Charleston.
Piss and vinegar. Sauce and scrap.
And yet she dips everything in honey.
Contradictions thick as molasses served like baked apples to a hungry child.

—*Elie Davis*

MY SOUTH SWAPS RECIPES WITH THE METER MAID WHILE SHE WRITES YOU A TICKET.

My South doesn't dab the '60s with sugar and spice.

My South is my home.
It's where I was born and raised like
my mother, and my grandmother,
and many past grandmothers.
It's where my children will rise up like the
Mississippi and give life to dreams that
past generations were afraid to dream.

My South is educated by trial and errors of
our ancestors, and refined in universities.
It is talk about good and evil in
small towns that want to be big cities
and concrete jungles that feel like small towns.

My South is *not* all about barbecue and blues.
It is sunset symphonies and fine wines and
high-class restaurants and southern R&B
so alive that you can't sit still and
gospel so good it brings you to tears.

—*Sierra Fitzgerald*

In my South, there were legs built to stand strong.

When all else had failed and anything could go wrong,

as a legacy of strength, they were made to carry on.

In my South, these legs have walked many miles.

They came in different shapes and sizes to fit any style.

But they have been worked and whipped, scarred and stripped.

Sores went neglected, ignored until infected.

But never once did they stop to rest.

As each burden was lashed out, they always did their best.

And no matter how hard the task, these legs were built to last.

From all over the world they traveled—

standing, fighting, for our freedom and rights.

They even walked through bad and stormy weather,

but never once lost their insight.

The March from Selma, to Montgomery, Alabama, was more than proof

to show that these legs had stamina.

So I'll take pride in knowin', and I don't mind showin',

these beautiful legs are mine.

Because they were handed down from ancestral times.

So oh, to these legs, you should stand proud when you see them coming.

For these are the legs of a strong southern woman.

—*Delores Smith*

IN MY
SOUTH,
THERE ARE
STILL DIRT
ROADS.

My South is nappy hair and straightenin' combs and plats, not braids.

It's family reunions and barbecues and fish fries.

And "God willin' and the creek don't rise."

Straight-out-of-the-oven sweet potato pie.

Homemade—never store-bought.

In my South, it's always "yes ma'am," "yes sir."

Respect your elders. Love your neighbors.

And if you don't have anything nice to say, don't say nothing at all.

'Cause as Big Mama told me: "God don't like ugly."

And there was something else my Big Mama told me:

"Home is where the heart is."

—*Avainti Dyer*

In my South, children fall asleep on parents' laps while sitting in rocking chairs made by their great-great-grandfathers.

My South is the cardinal's song and the flight of a hummingbird.

A rookery filled with fledgling egrets.

A doe as it grazes with its fawn on the highway's edge.

Raccoon tracks beside the garbage bin.

A blue jay nest hidden among the ivy.

My South is the parade of double daylilies along a country road.

A camellia blossom afloat in a crystal bowl.

The perfume of wisteria in April.

The antique rose from my grandmother's house.

A red canna lily with leaves like those of the banana tree.

It's the scent of four-o'clocks on an August afternoon.

—*Frances Pierce*

In my South,
the most treasured things passed down
from generation to generation
are the *family recipes.*

Carl Jones

My South knows that *To Kill a Mockingbird* is the best work of fiction ever written,
the sweetest peaches grow in the backyard,
and vacation is always a week at the beach—Myrtle Beach.
Same hotel every year, meals included.

In my South, the showiest flowers bloom in the dead of winter.
Early spring's perfectly warm days reappear in late fall.
And in summer, cotton is still king, at least in sultry summer seersucker.

In my South, we like to reminisce.
Sometimes I can go back forty years in my mind's eye to those sultry summer days,
when the northern cousins came to visit for weeks and we swam all day at the lake,
relished eating a picnic of banana sandwiches with mayo on white bread,
and Aunt Nellie told me, at least once a day, that I would grow up to be Miss America.

In my South, of today, I cherish my garden, the cedar waxwings who come to chat
and eat my holly berries, the shade of a two-hundred-year oak offered graciously, three lazy cats
stretched out a mile long on the porch, and a banana sandwich with mayo on white bread.

—Debbie Scott

My South is old Savannah, its cemeteries crowded with tourists—the dust jackets of *Midnight in the Garden of Good and Evil* peeking out of their Gucci tote bags.

My South is hot.

Not that nice dry breezy hot,

but that so hot you feel like

you can't breathe.

Shirt-stuck-to-your-sweaty-skin hot.

—*Melody Cook*

Carl Jones

My South
has
majestic oaks
that have
healed
over
time from
the wounds
of war
and the
advancement
of man.

Carl Jones

In my South, gettin' too big for your britches has nothing to do with how much fried chicken or pie you had to eat.

I mean it's nice to be important, but we don't like people that are too big for their britches, now do we?

A smile is expected, even when you're going through a world of hurt.

Someone will unfailingly say to you "bless you" if you sneeze and they will also say "bless your heart" if you act like an idiot.

—*Christine Carr*

In my South,
Johnny Cash will never die as long as
I'm still wearin' black!

My South is Nanna's house, a big, white, painted brick house filled with antiques.
It has a wide front porch with a swing.
The swing has a rusted chain with one side about two lengths longer than the other—
makes you kind of slide to one end.
It's the same swing that my daddy proposed to my mama in thirty years ago.
Nanna makes us sit there after she's been to the farmer's market—to shuck corn and shell peas.
And all the grandkids pitch in 'cause if we don't, we can't eat.

At dinner we sit at the oval oak table set with the good china and silver.
We sit here every Sunday, holiday, birthday, engagement, marriage, birth, and death.
Aunt Roberta sits across from me, her white hair like a bushy helmet, hard with Aqua Net.
She shakes her hands wildly and points as she recounts the latest horrific murders heard on CNN,
breaking the worst parts with, "Hon, could you pass the okra?"
And everyone smiles because we know we'll miss her when she's gone.

My South is family.
Between everyone in my family by birth or marriage, we're related to all of Alabama
and at least half of Tennessee.
Home is anywhere a Brown, Holman, Hedge, or Shaefer said it was.
Home is what we defended in the wars, but most of all, my South is Nanna and Papa.
Magic. Balloon animals. Sewing.
Pictures of sixty years of marriage.
And corn bread on Sunday.

—Allison Shaefer Brown

In my South, grandmothers are called "Mimi,"
"Damma," "Bubber," and "Spook."

My South is runnin' barefoot through sweet soft zoysia grass.

Catchin' lightnin' bugs in a Mason jar.

And summer so hot you can break a sweat just thinkin'.

Nights so still and thick and hot that ya flop and

ya flop and ya flop.

Just like a crappie lookin' for the cool spot.

As a child playin' in a hose, makin' sunshine rainbows and sittin' in

the yard with fifteen cents in hand waiting to buy a sky-blue

Popsicle from the ice-cream man.

—Kathleen (KC) Jensen

My South was cane-pole fishing and creek swimming.

My South is
*the Grand Strand, Ocean Drive,
bumper-to-bumper beach goers,
elbow-to-elbow high-rise condos.*

My South is a place where when tomorrow is
Easter Sunday and you ain't got no money,
the barber tell you, "Boy, get up in my chair
and don't even look at your wallet."
And y'all still listen to the Braves on that
same AM radio he heard Hank break
Babe's record back in 1974 on.
Where old folks, on the front porch, with their
gold teeth laughin'—it's like the sweet, sweet sound
of the gate's of heaven swingin'.
And uncles trim their front yard hedges,
waving to every car that passes by.
And "Last time I see you girl, you was this high."

—Ayodele Heath

In my South, you have a pickup truck.
Well, you may have several, but you have one that works.
You'll wash it exactly twice.
The day after you buy it and the day before you sell it.
When it breaks you jack it up in the driveway
and fix it yourself.
If you can't fix it, you replace the jacks with genuine made-
in-the-South masonry cylinder blocks—and you move on.
But usually you get her patched up.
When you're young you do this because you usually have
the time and because you're broke.
When you're old you do it because it makes you
feel young—and because you're broke.
Plus, it's entirely possible that you bust your knuckles open
on the exhaust manifold.
Then you can kind of walk back in the house all greasy
and bloody—tell your old lady you fixed the truck.
In my South, that impresses women.
At the very least you'll get supper brought to you in the
recliner while you watch *Andy*.
That's two out of three on a perfect evening scorecard—
in my South.

—*David Bird*

Frances McBrien

My South
remembers
a humble king,
lift every voice
and sing, and
let freedom ring

And I know in my South there is a link between family and land,

of human lives sacrificed in it, because a sense of place is that important.

I also know that at the end of my life I will have been made whole by this place,

and I will feel that swell behind the eyes as I last look at the setting sun as it

bullions out into pinks and purples and yellow.

I will look back and I'll remember the taste of spring honeysuckle air,

the fine lines of the blue heron in the marsh,

and Mom's homemade blackberry pies cooling in the window,

and how those berries would explode in our mouths a little brighter,

because we were the ones who picked them.

And one day I'll look back on this life and I won't wonder anymore.

—*Sean Scapaletto*

My South is *more than a place on the map.*

In my South, you don't have to be famous to be celebrated.

You don't have to have a lot of gas to really go somewhere.

You don't have to be rich to live a rich life.

In my South, you don't need much to have it all.

—*Charlie Geer*

My South is *my heart.*

125

ATLANTA

Consultant   Kodac Harrison

Venues   Java Monkey, Decatur—Michael Gallagher
          Oglethorpe University—Chad Yarborough

Judges   Megan Sexton
          Stephen Goforth
          Belinda Skelton

BIRMINGHAM

Consultants   Derico Dabney
               Lindsay Stone
               Kirk Hardesty
               La Shanna Price

Venues   Carver Theatre—Leah Tucker
          SOBO—Al Rabiee
          High Note—Sam Pilato
          Workplay—Michael Panepento

Judges   Hunter Bell
          BBrian
          Gwen DeRu
          Bob Collins
          Alicia Johnson-Reed
          Dale Short
          Kim Moore
          Alec Harvey

CHARLESTON

Consultants   Ellie Davis
               Harold Singletary
               Paul Allen

Venues   LJ's—Chuck
          Port City Java—Witt Langstaff
          Bar 145
          US Custom House—Connie Bays

Judges   Nickie Hardin
          Tanya Brown
          Baby J and Tessa
          Lorne Chambers
          Susan Myers
          Kwami Daws
          Marjory Wentworth
          Richard Garcia

Kyle Christy/Turner South

CHARLOTTE

Consultants
: Benjamin (JC) Cowan
Jessica Deltac

Venues
: McGlohon Theatre at Spirit Square—
Lynn Price, Paul Setzer
The Evening Muse—Joe & Leah Kuhlmann

Judges
: Ann Lambert
Chuck Sullivan
Toni-B

MEMPHIS

Consultants
: Thom Holcomb
Brotha's Keepa—J'Malo & Ed

Venues
: Java Cabana—Mary Burns
Java, Juice & Jazz—Antwoinette
(Tony) Gilcrest
Precious Cargo
High Point—Bud Chittom

Judges
: La Kesh Hollingshed
Ruby O'Gray
Russell Coleman
Drew McCraven
Richard Thomspon
Alice Faye Duncan
Judy Dorsey
Bianca Phillips
Sophia Watkins
Mother Wit

Jake Herrle/Turner South

For Turner South

General Manager 1999–2004	David Rudolph
General Manager 2005–	Tom Karsch
VP, Marketing and On-Air	Pat Smith
Director of On-Air Production and New Ventures	Craig McMahon
Executive Producers	Sonny Del Grosso
	Craig McMahon
	Kevin Wagner
Line Producer	Carl Maduri
Production Coordinator	Jonathan Delgado
Photo Editors	Shana Lee
	Allison Katanich

IN MY SOUTH,
NEIGHBORS ARE MORE
THAN JUST THE PEOPLE
WHO LIVE NEXT DOOR.